Get The
Buck up
and Color
me

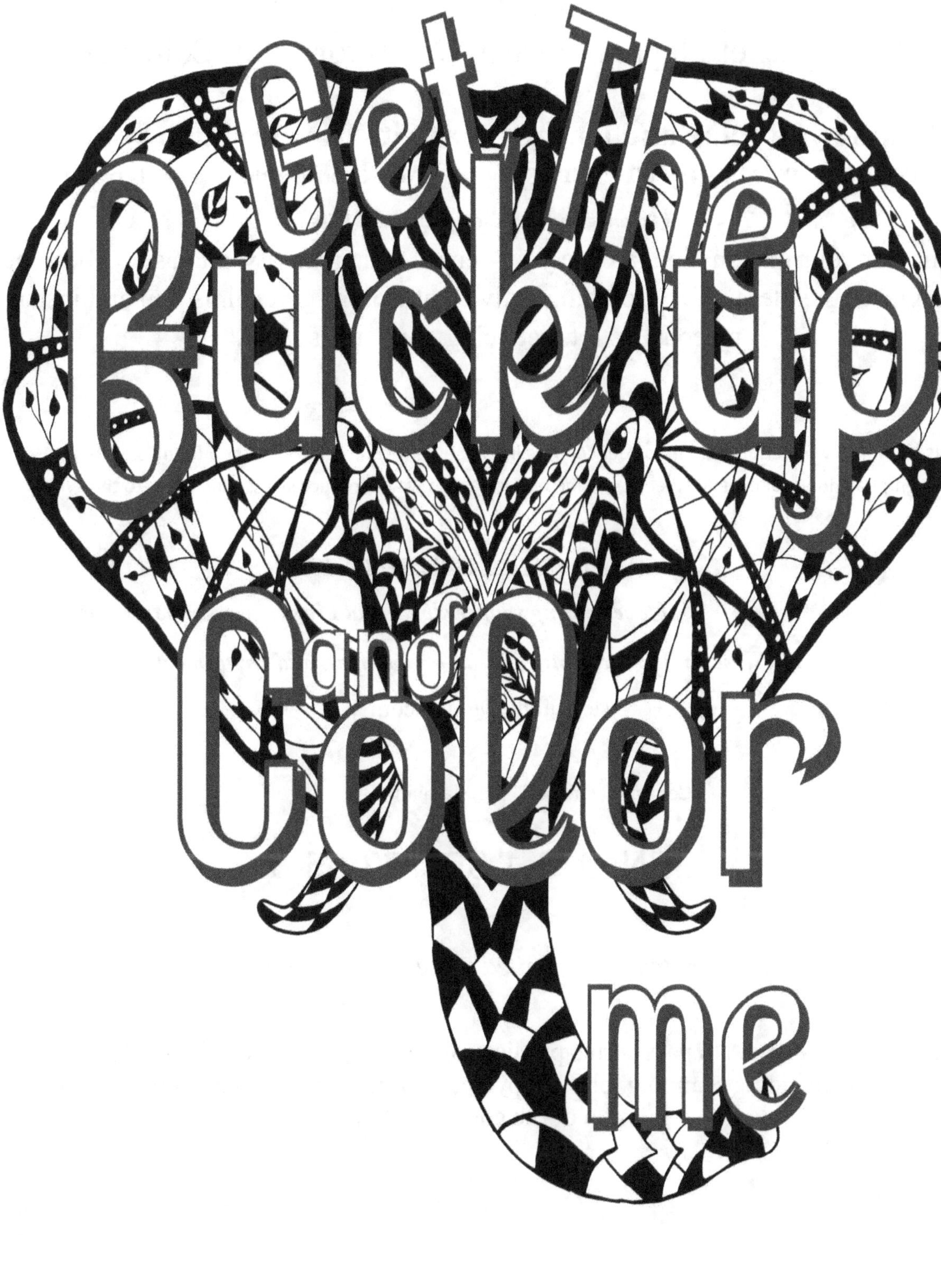

Swear Word
Stress Relief Elephant Swear Words for Adult Coloring!

It is time you relax and let the creativity flow through you. Step away from everyday life stress by taking Your Coloring to the Next Level - Learn the Art of Coloring and Achieve the Ultimate Bliss!

Bring out your imagination, arouse your senses and creativity, and as you become engaged in the pleasurable, soothing activity of Coloring, it calms you and instantaneously starts reducing your stress level.

This book is a wonderful addition to your coloring library; a perfect funny gag gift for a friend's birthday, Hen Night, Valentines or even Mother's Day, and a much easier way to reduce stress than going to the gym.

THANKS YOU FOR YOUR PATRONAGE

I love hearing your feedback and I read every single review

Please send your comment, ideas, compliments and anything else to me at:

stevojionu@gmail.com

Copyright © 2020, By: Mainland Publisher

ISBN: 978-1-950772-85-8

Printed in the United States of American

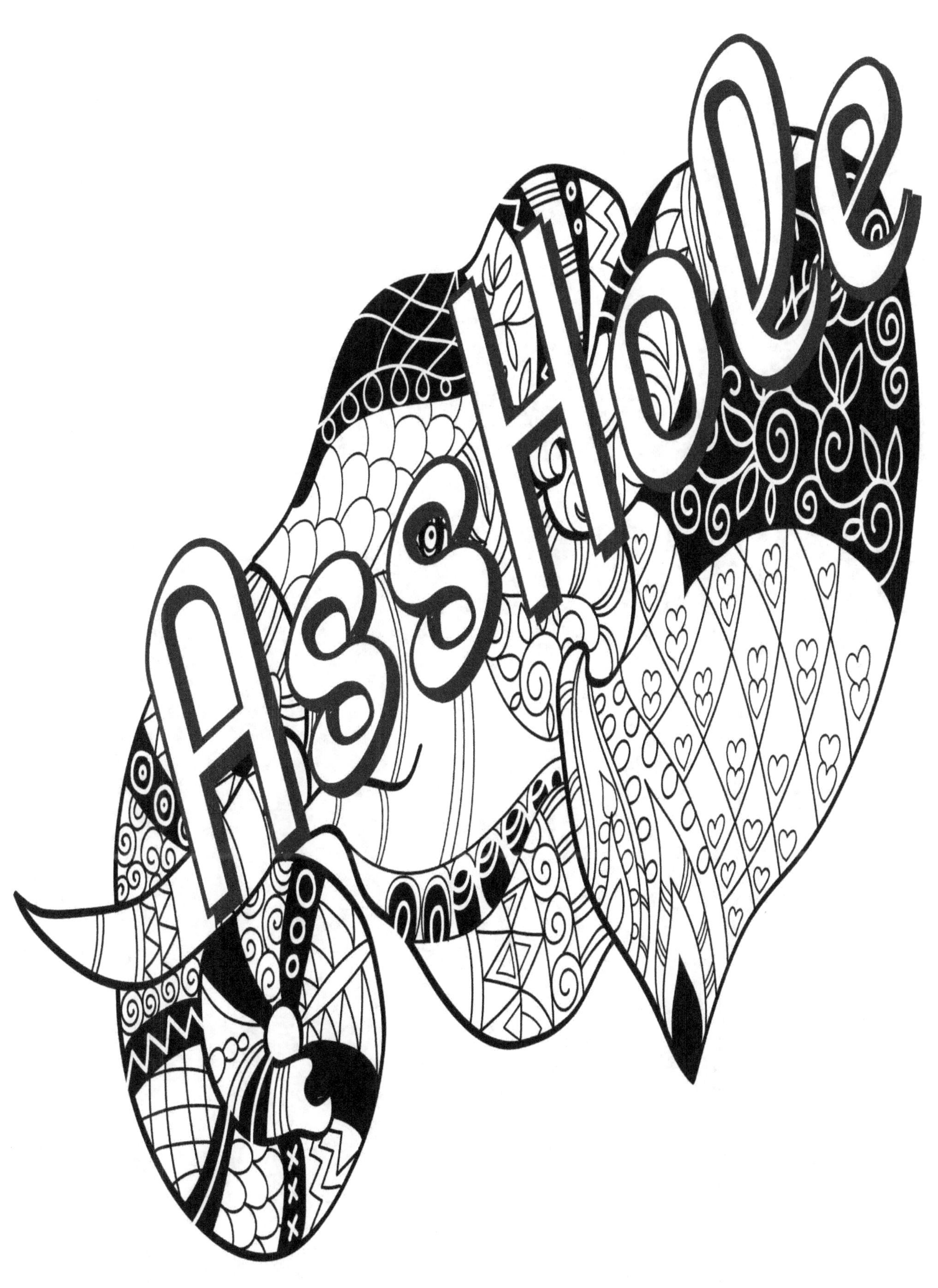
ASSHOLE

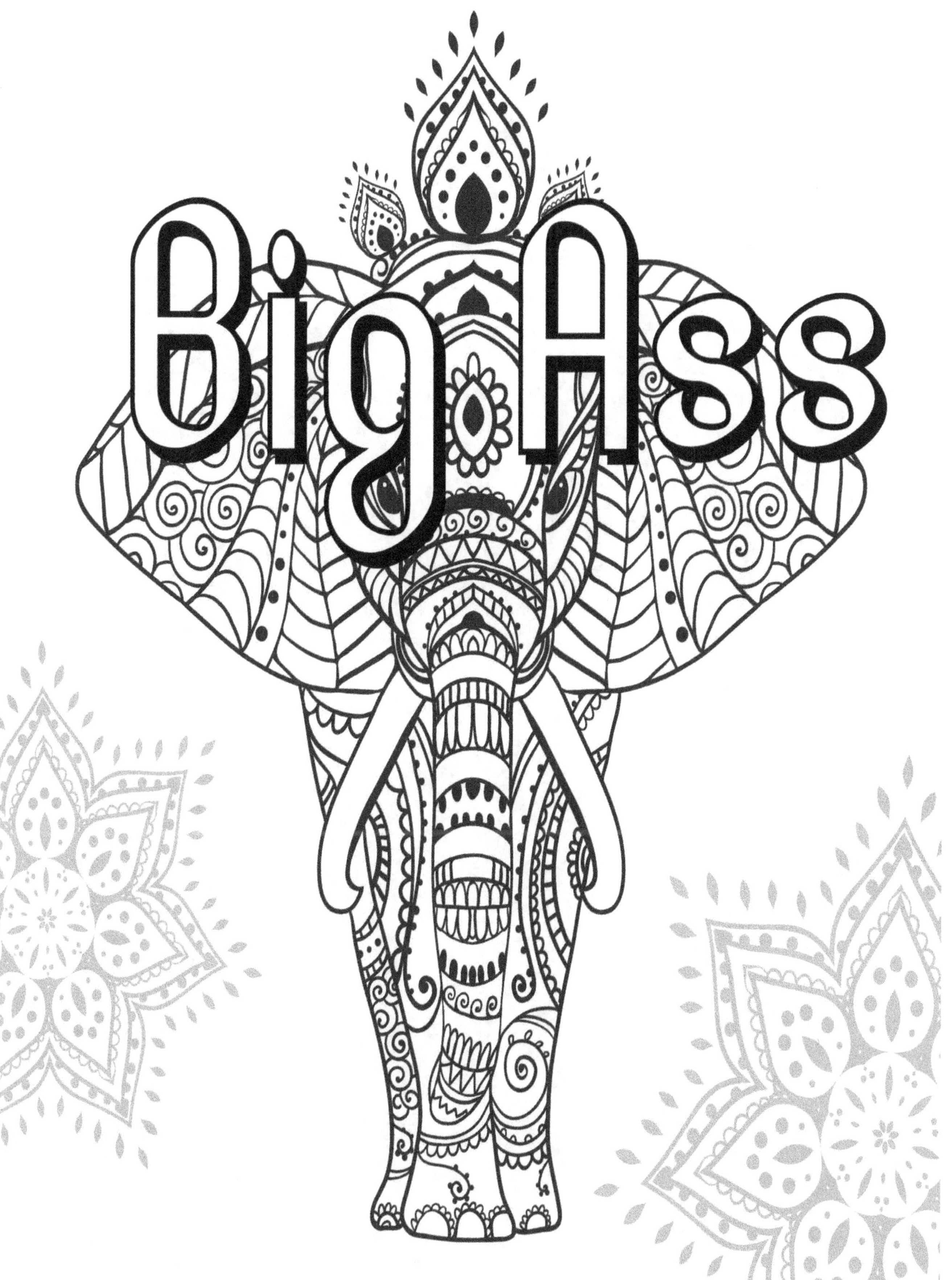

Big Ass

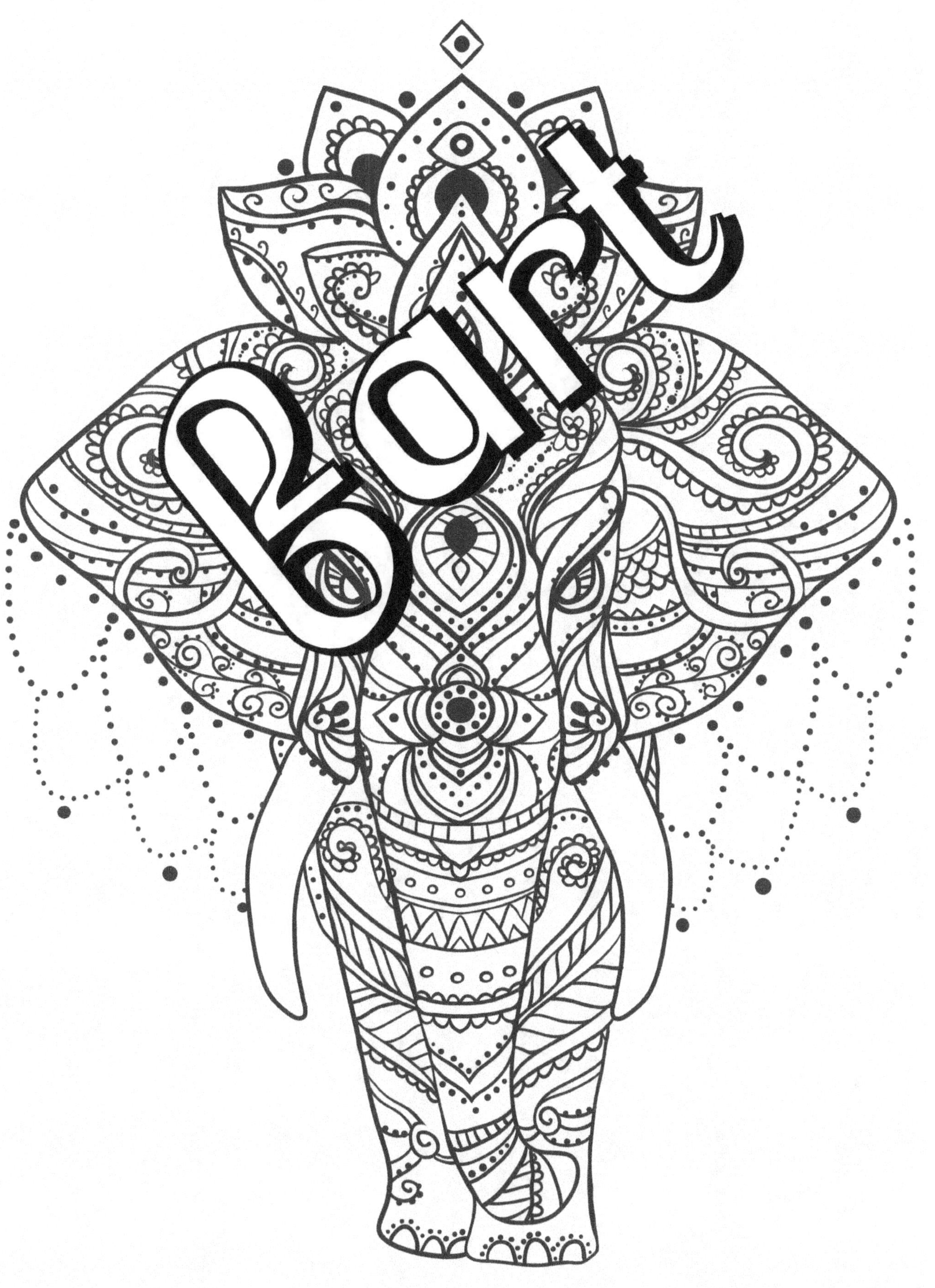
Bart

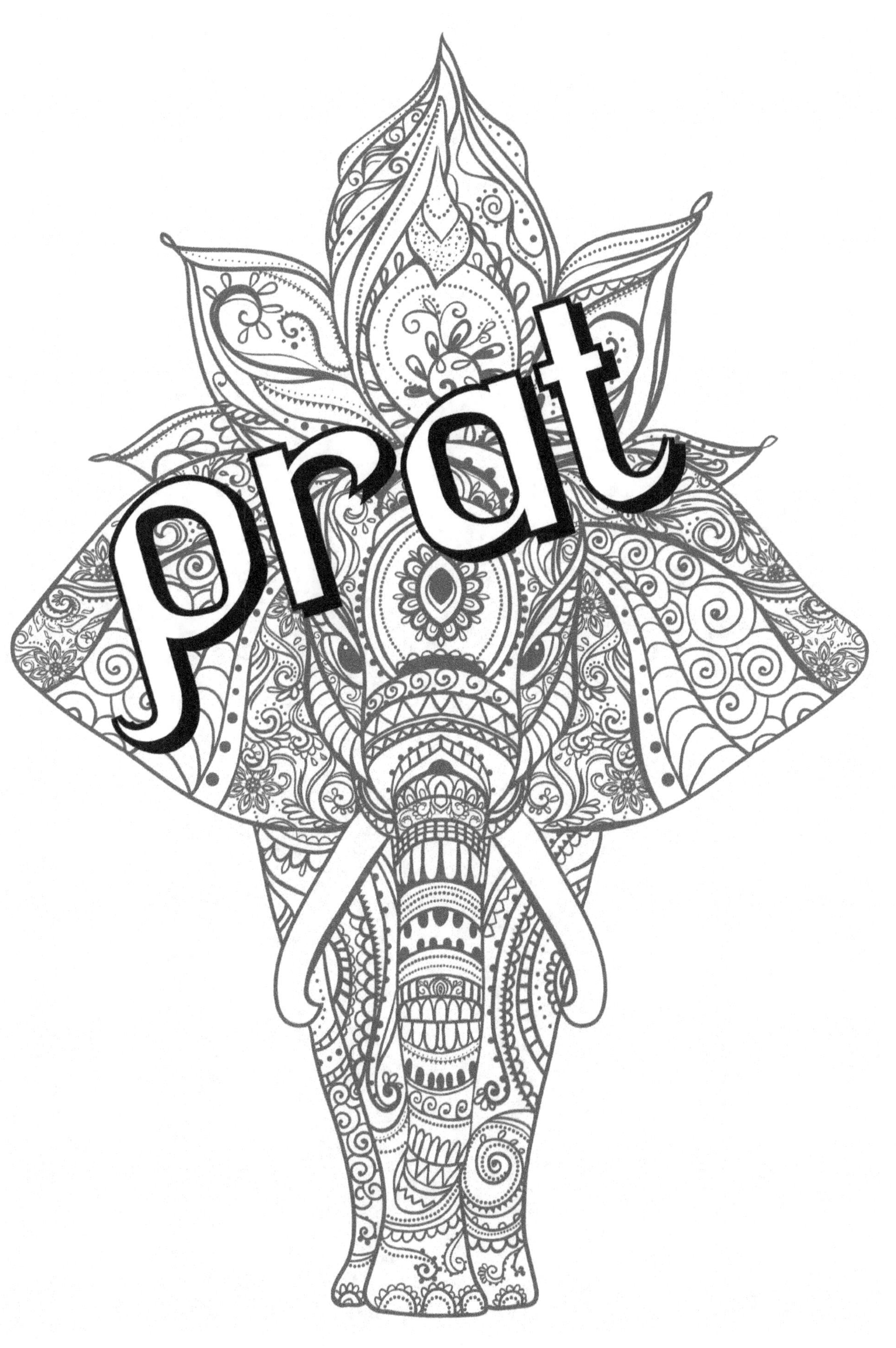
prat

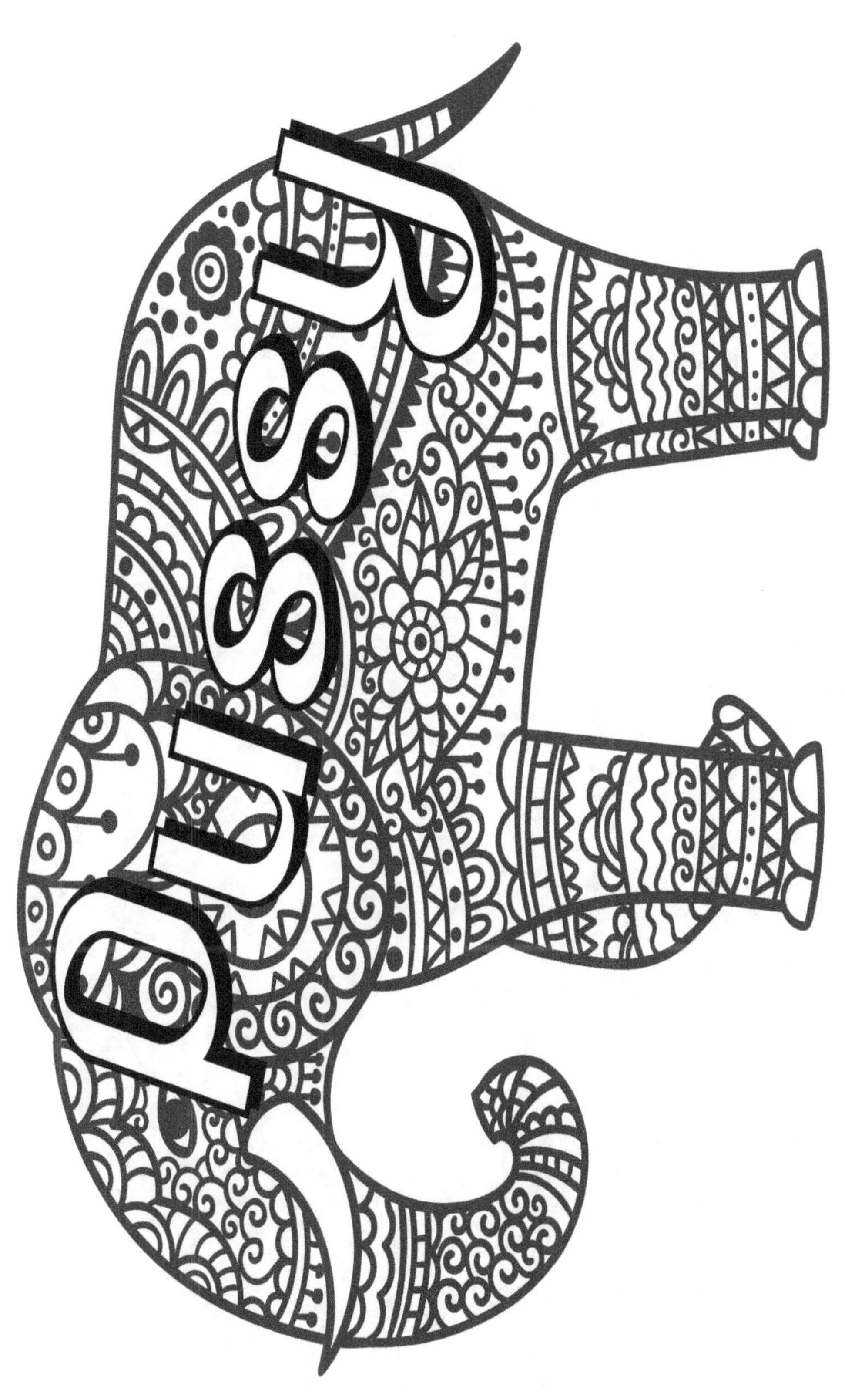

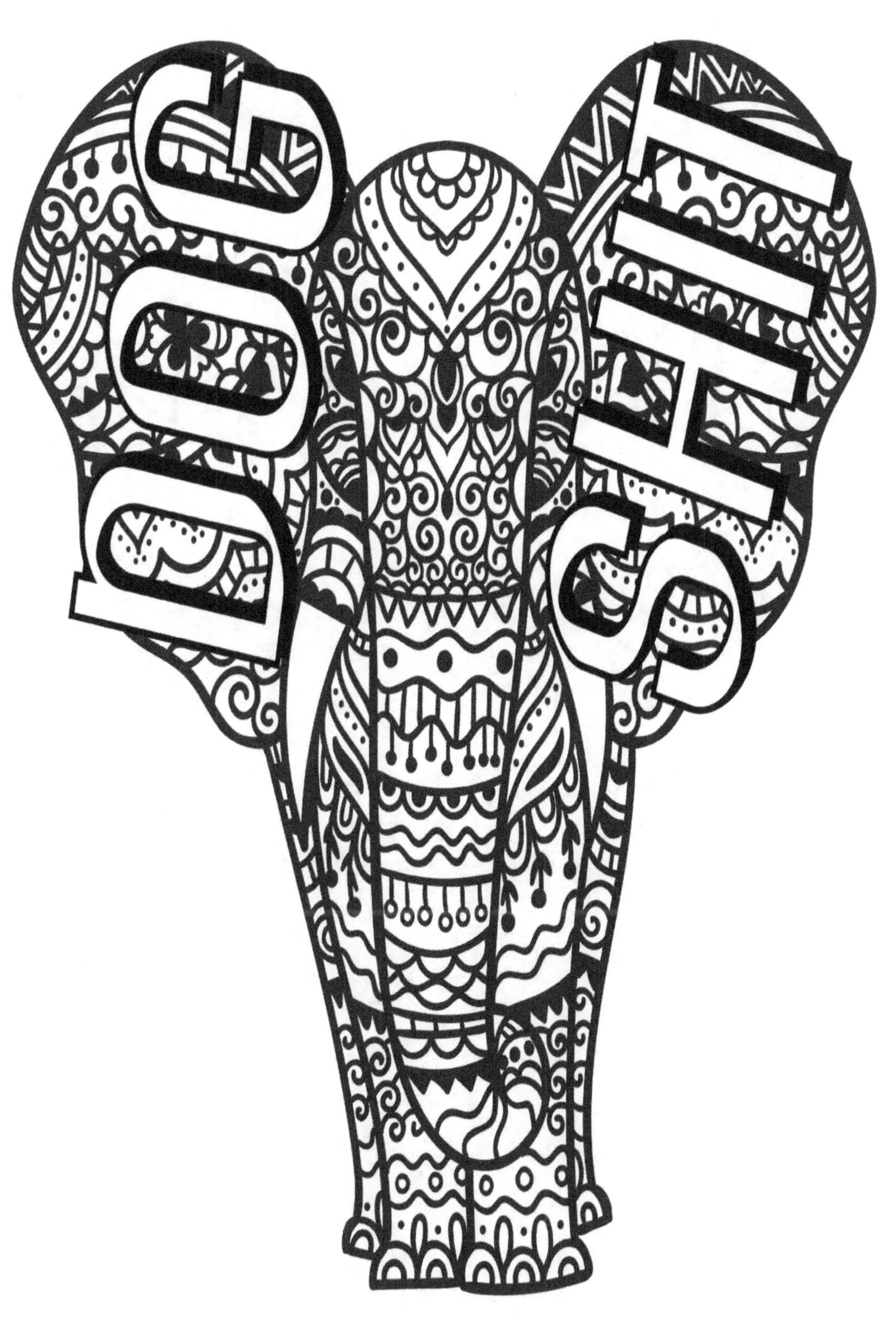

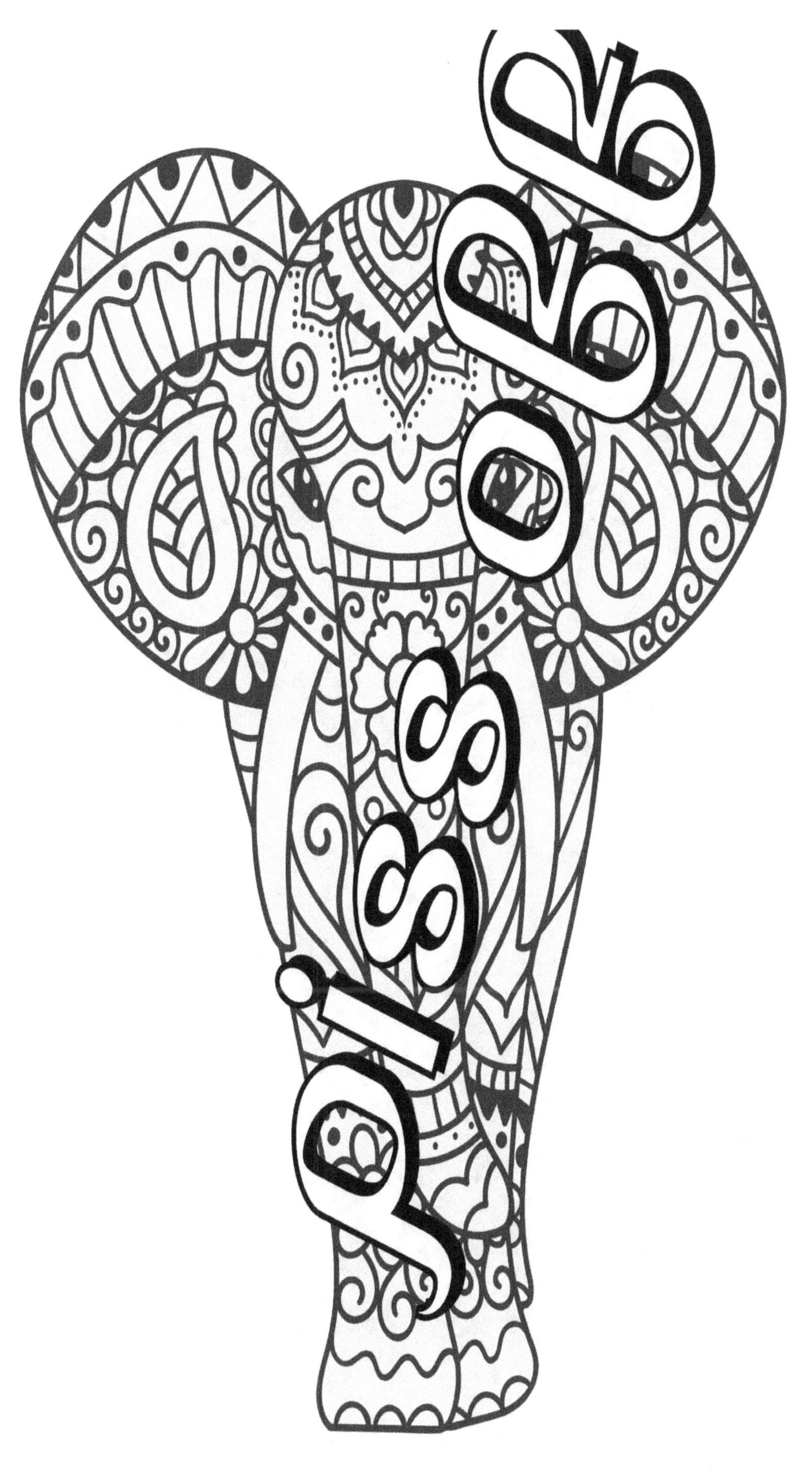

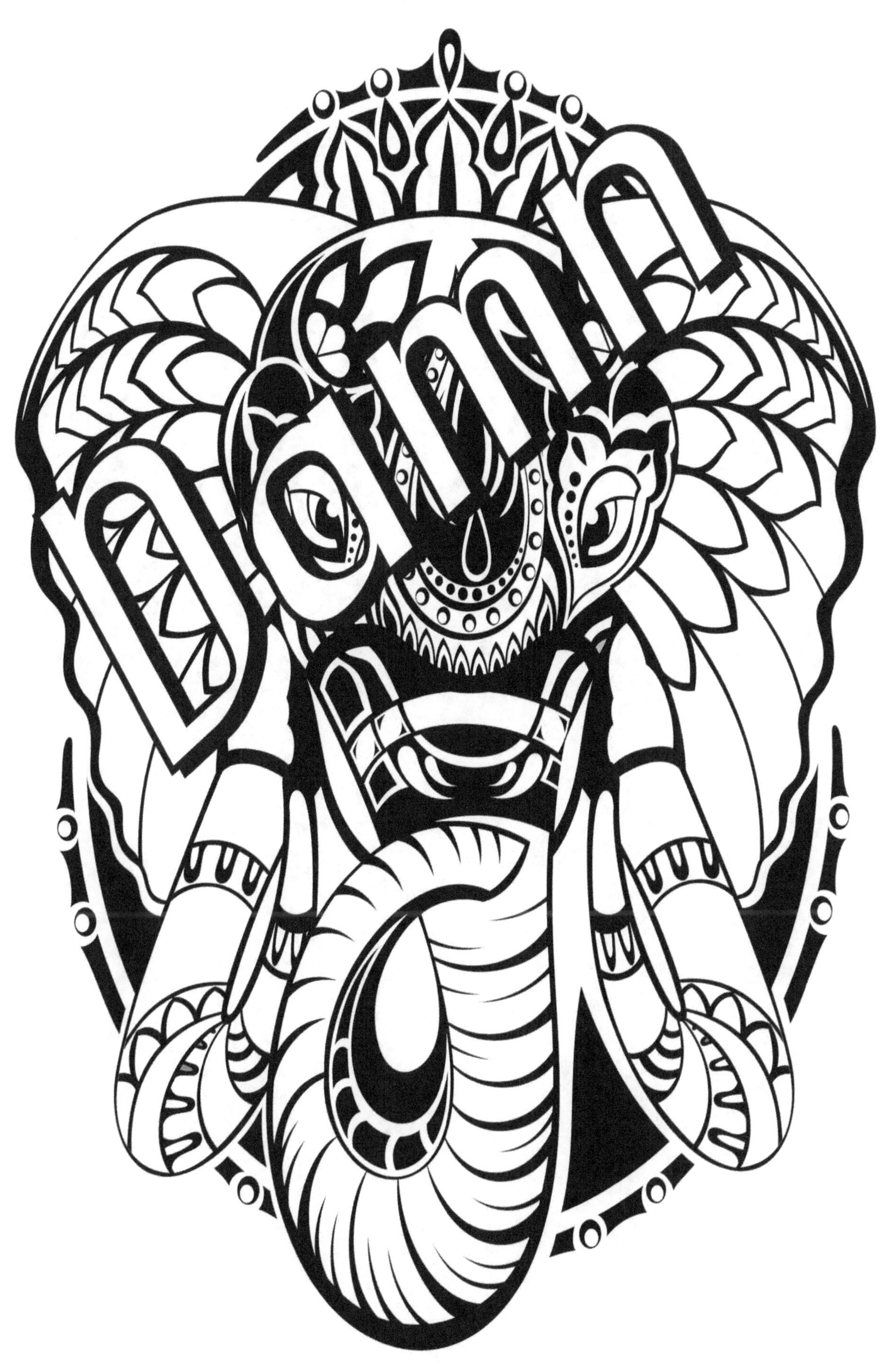
Damn

bloody hell

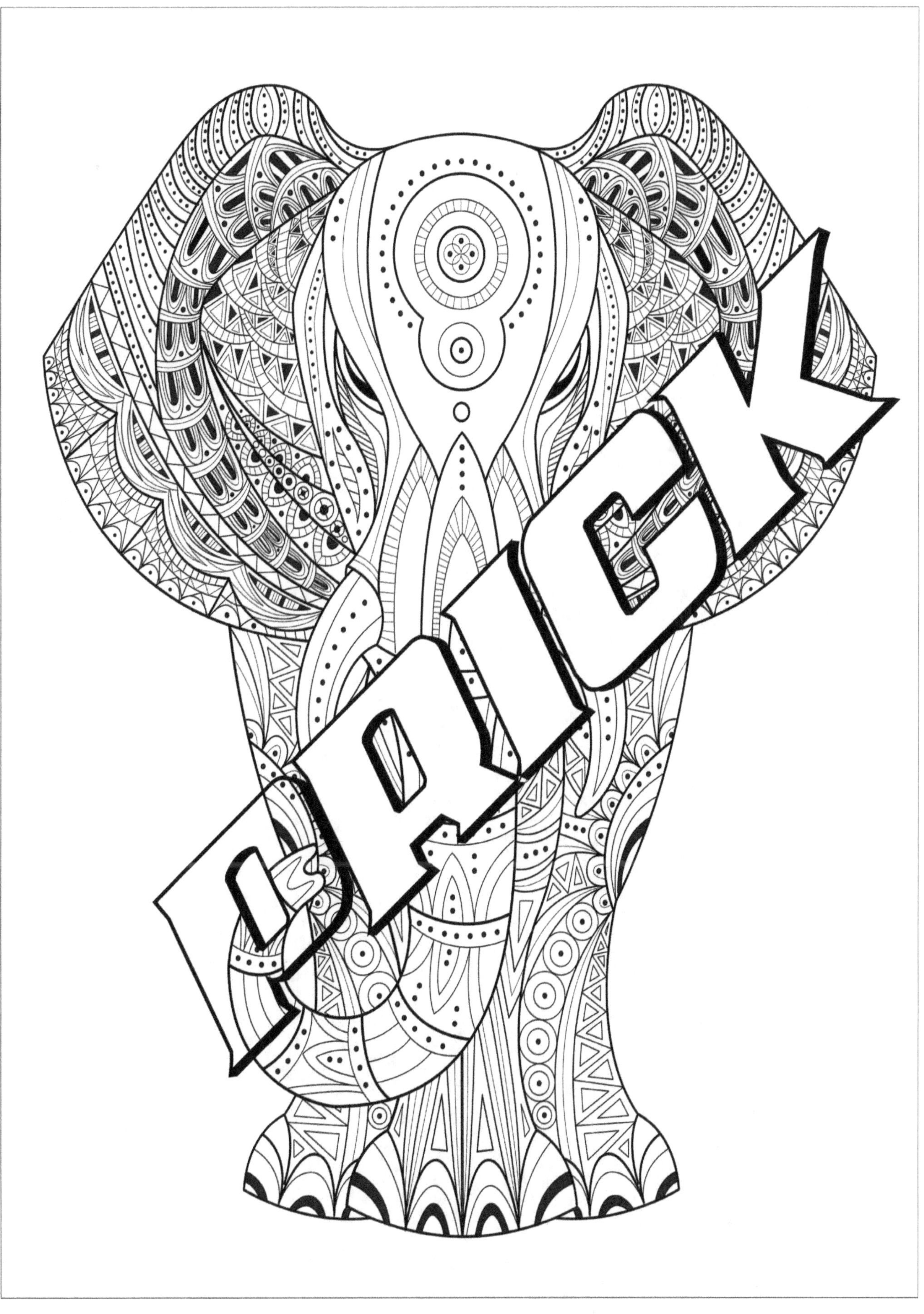
PRICK

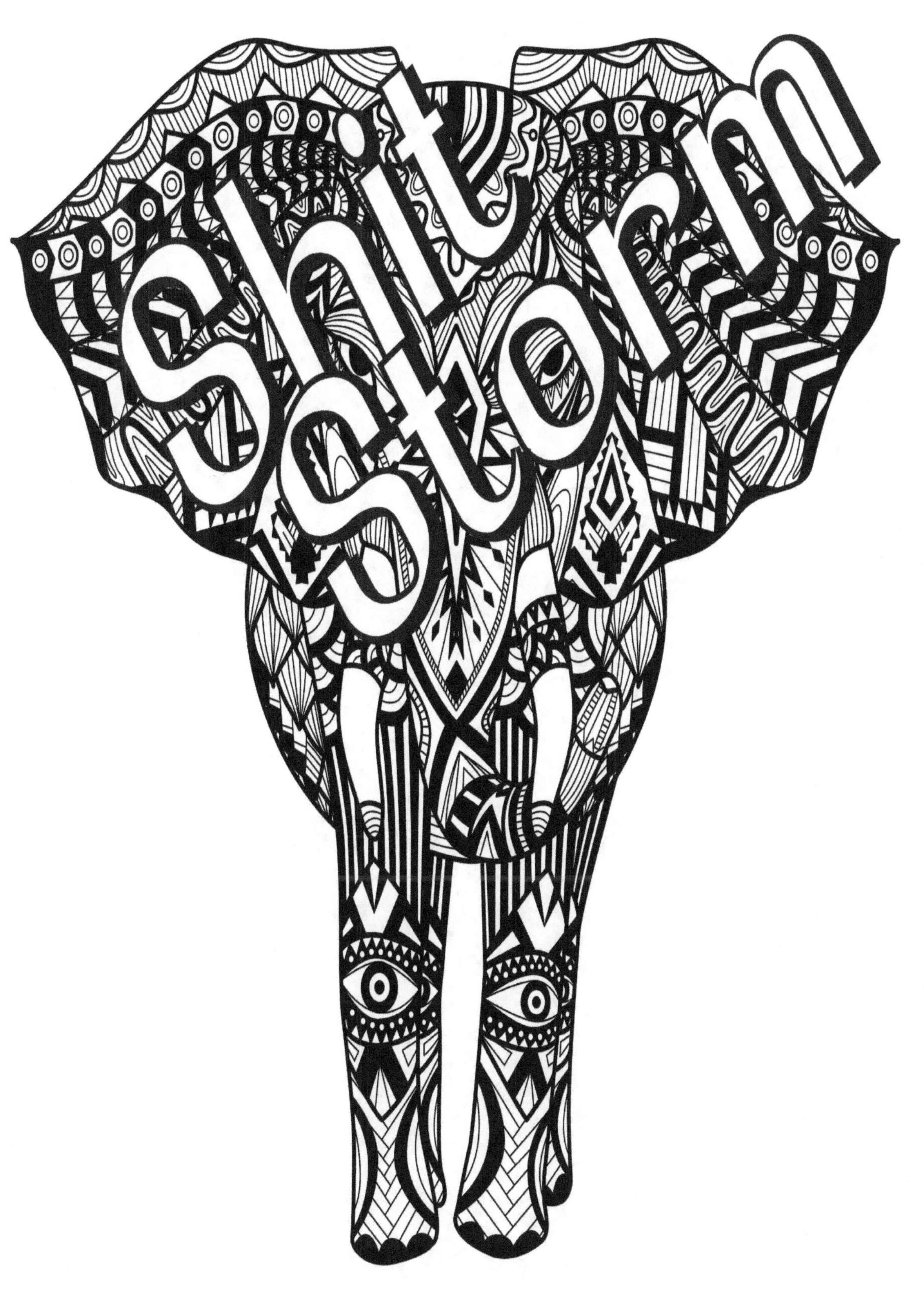

shit
storm

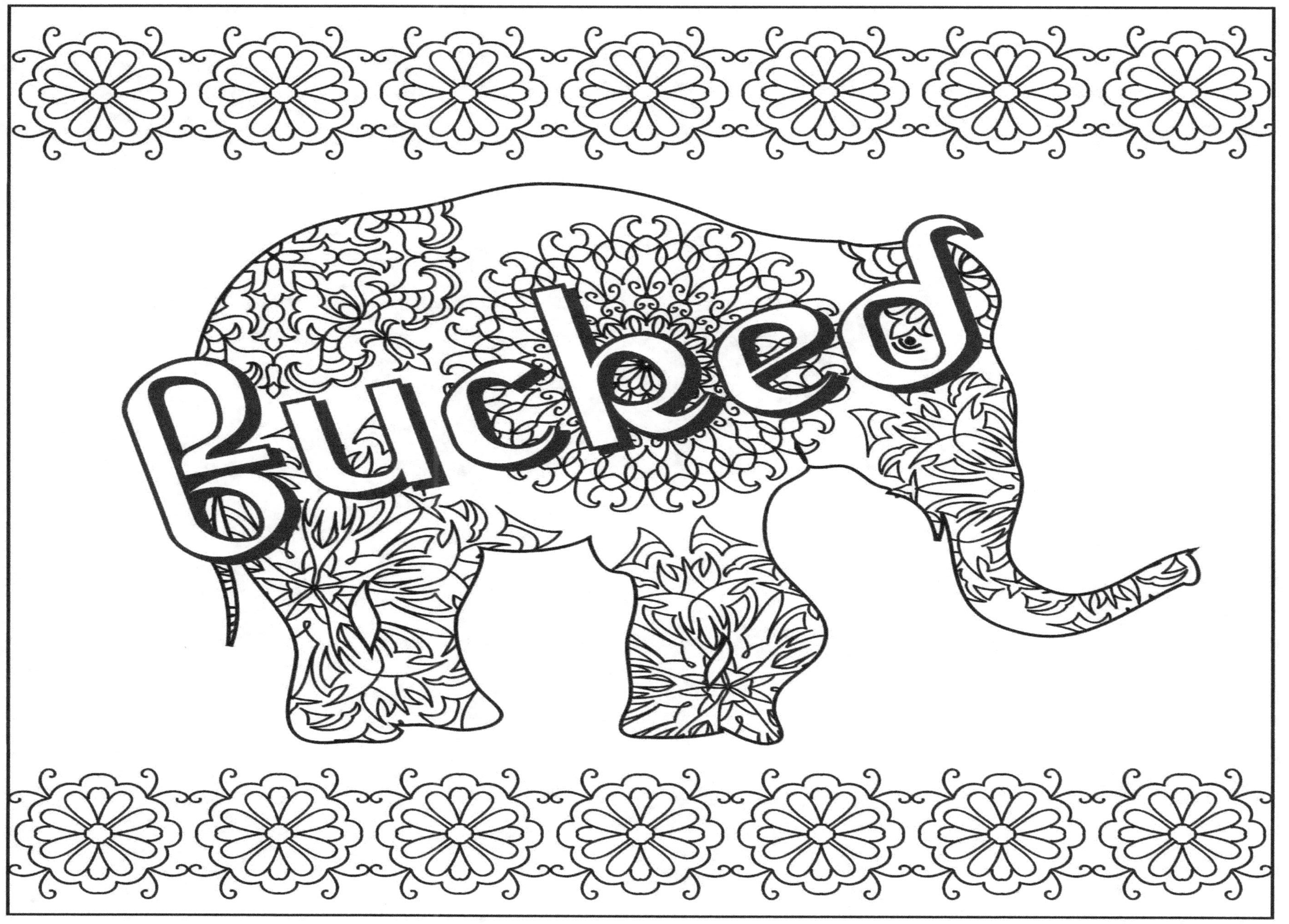
Bucked

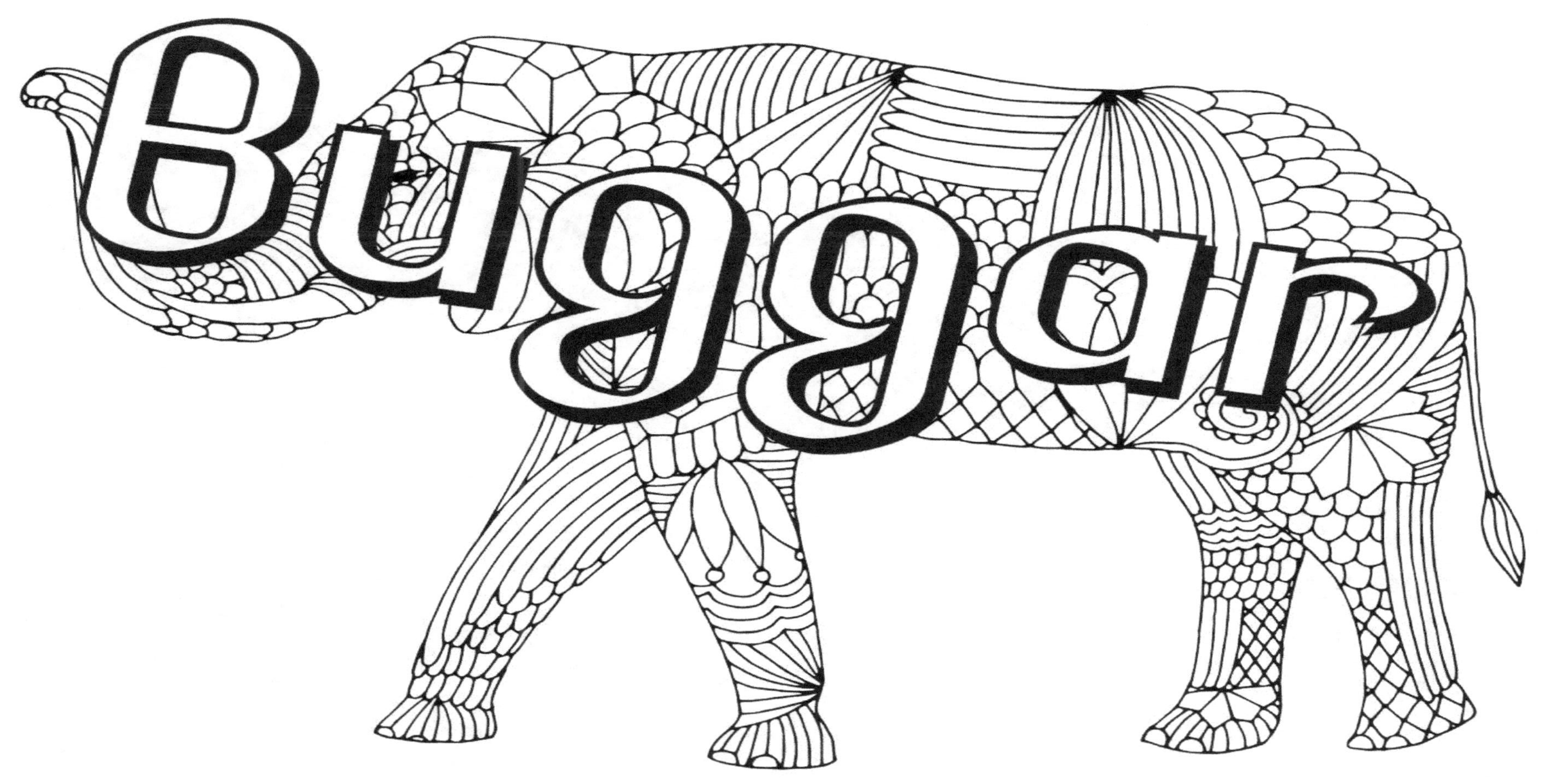
Buggar

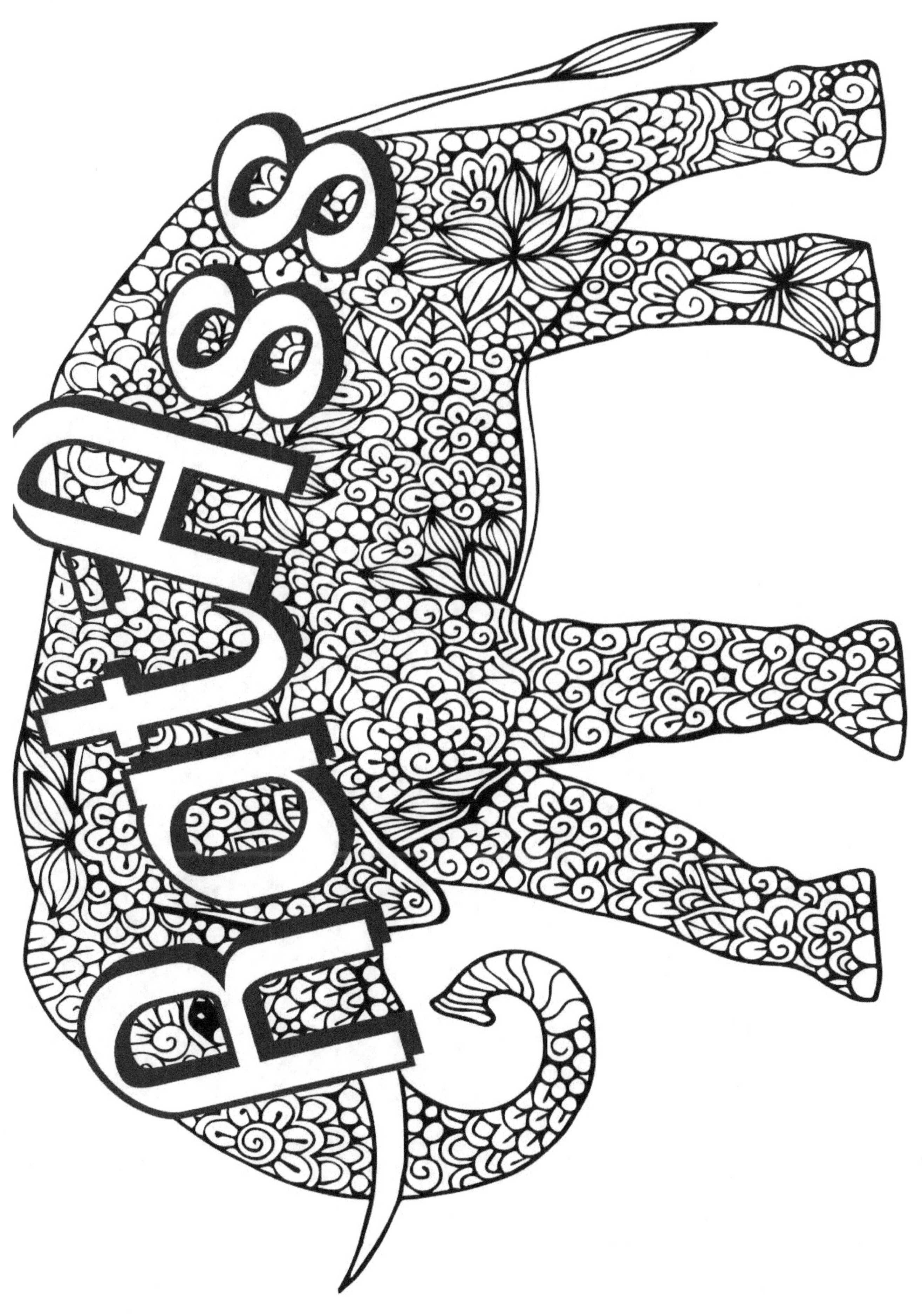

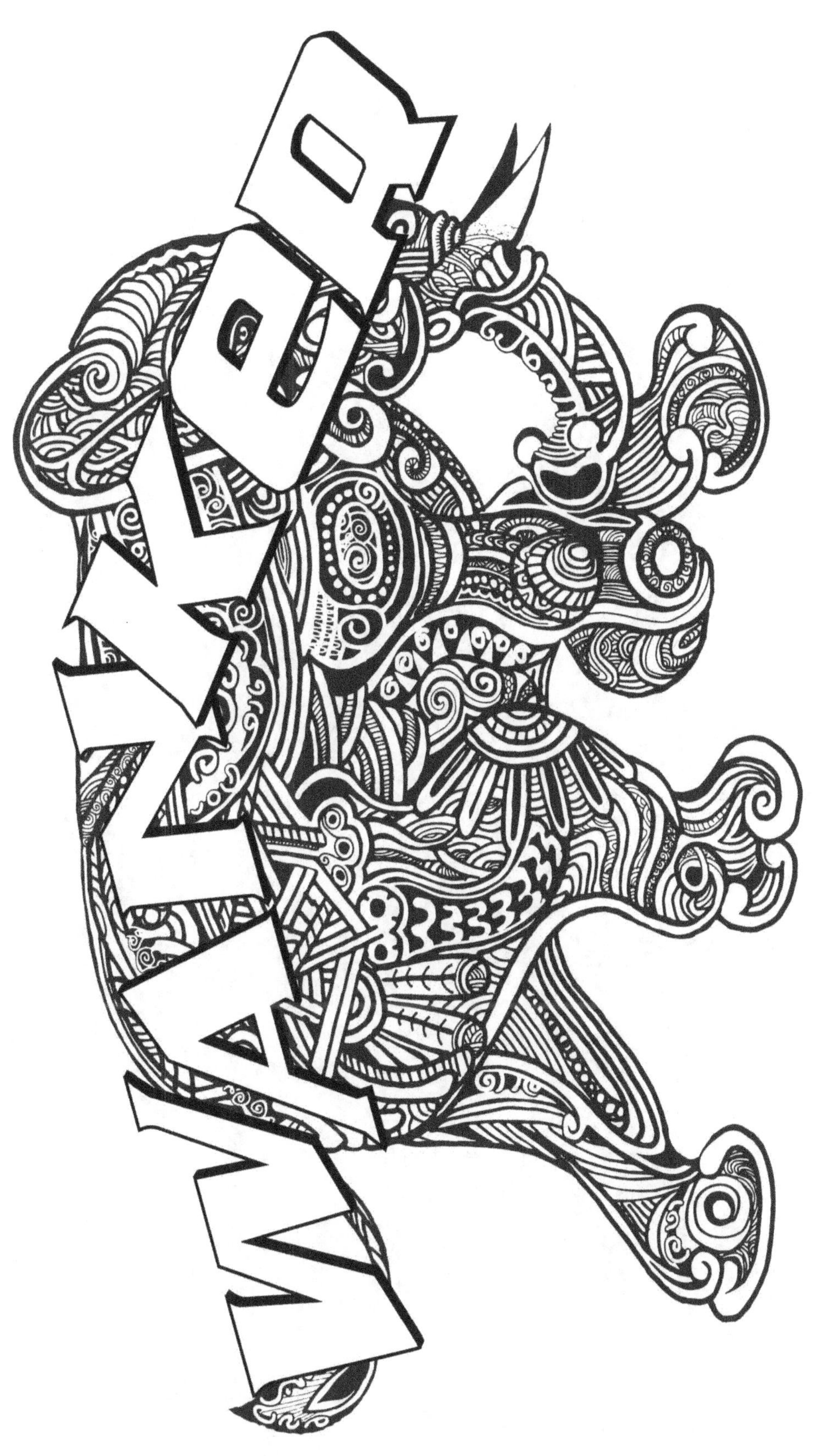
WANKER

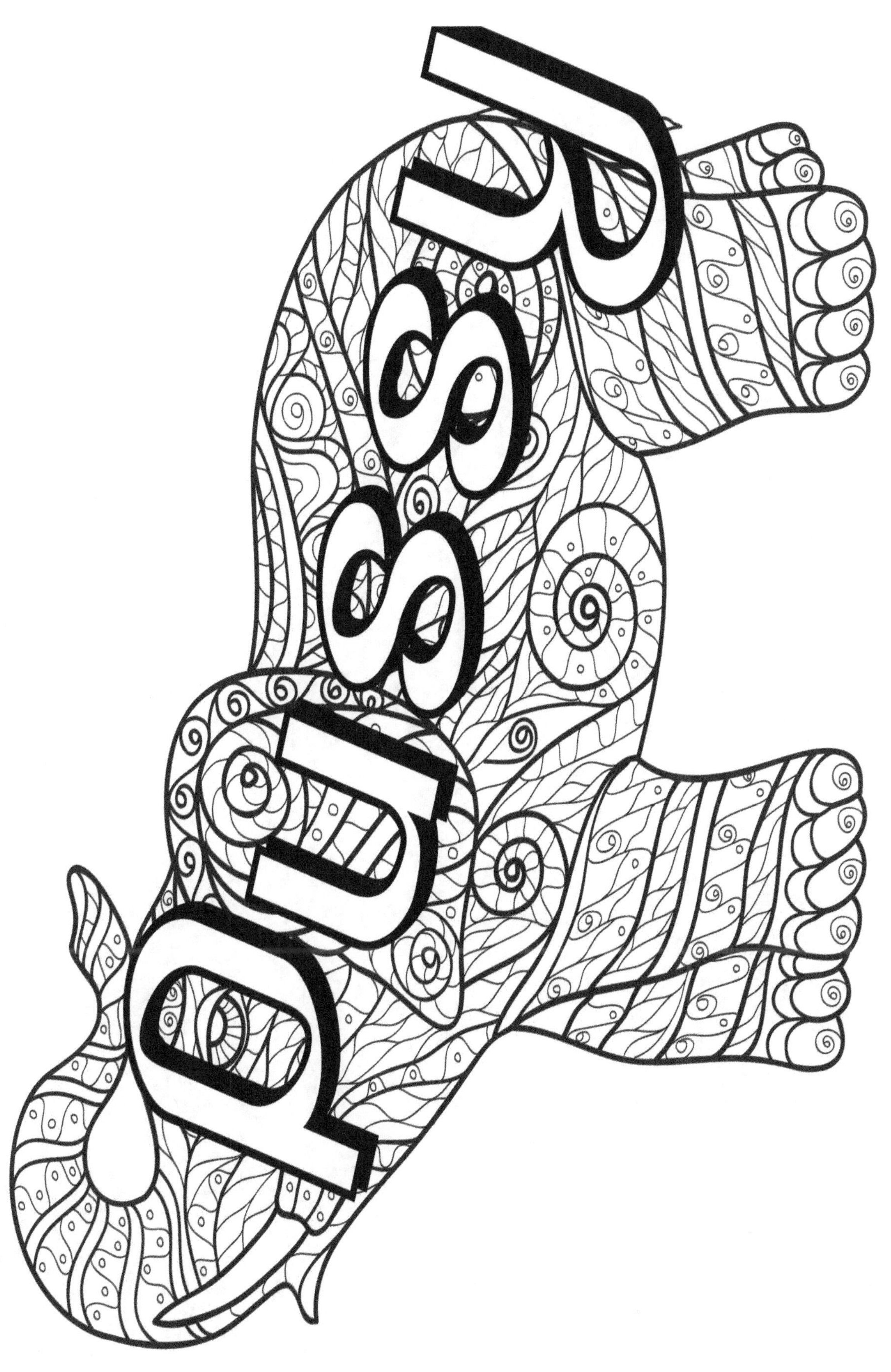

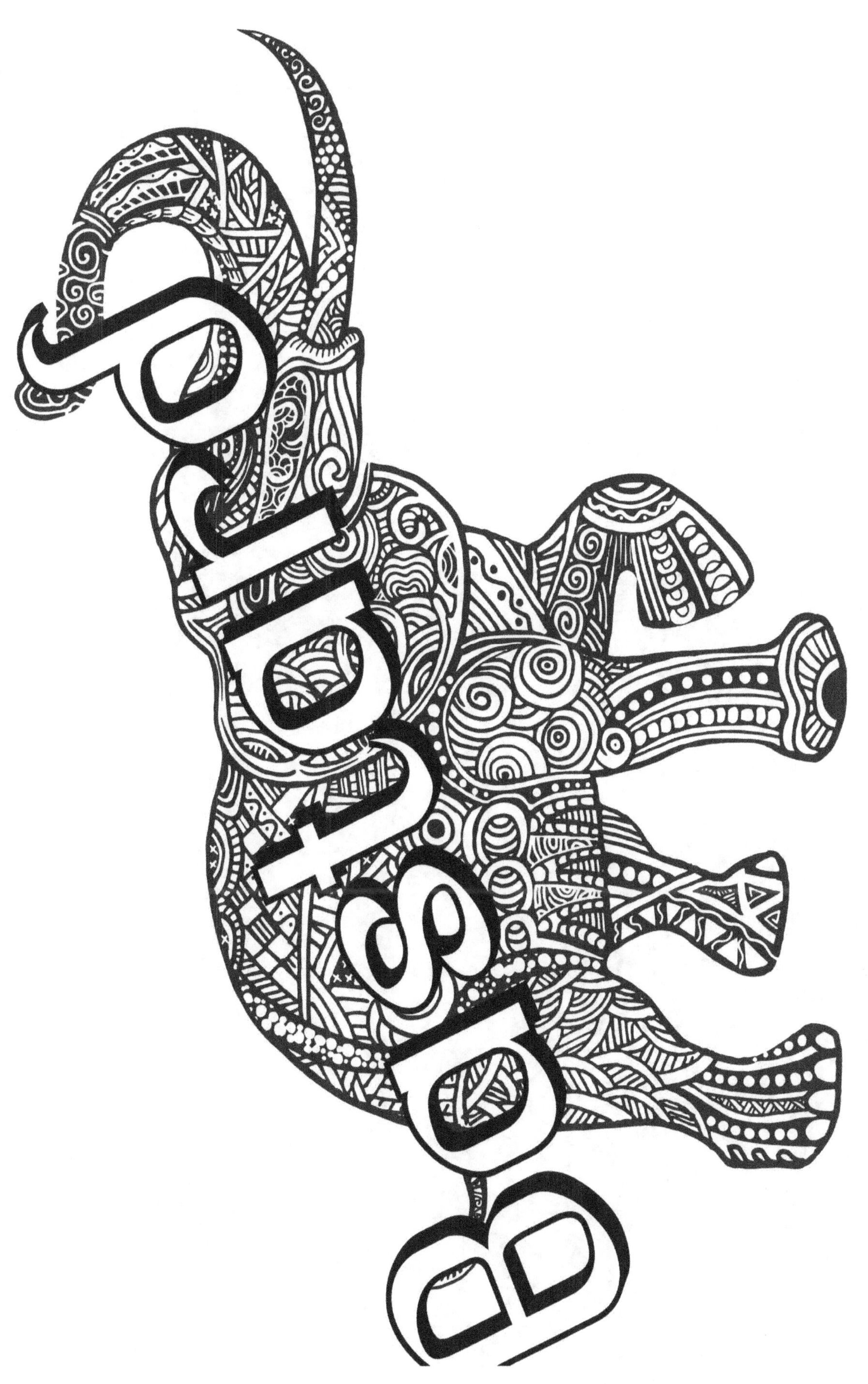

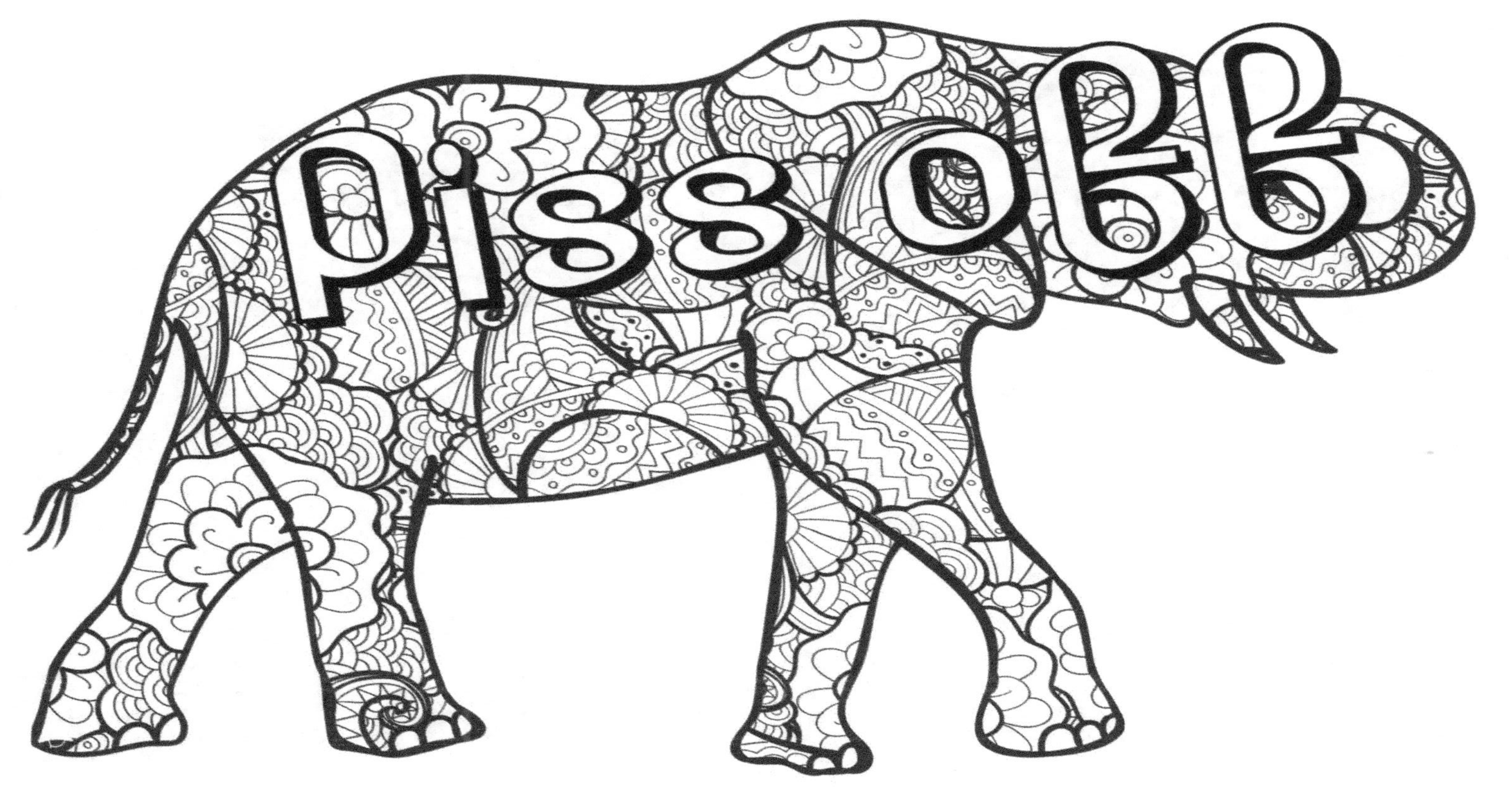
piss off

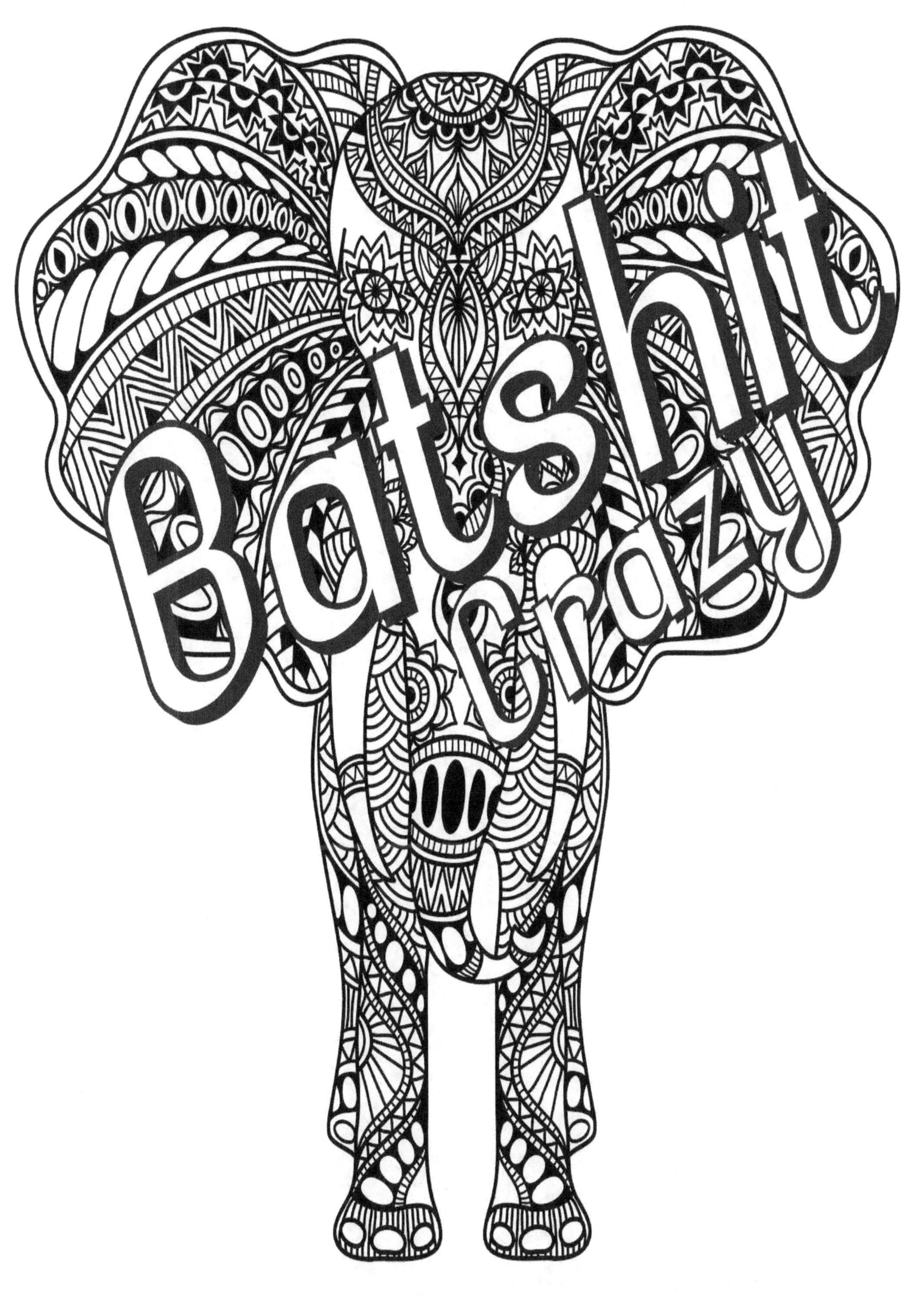

Batshit
Crazy

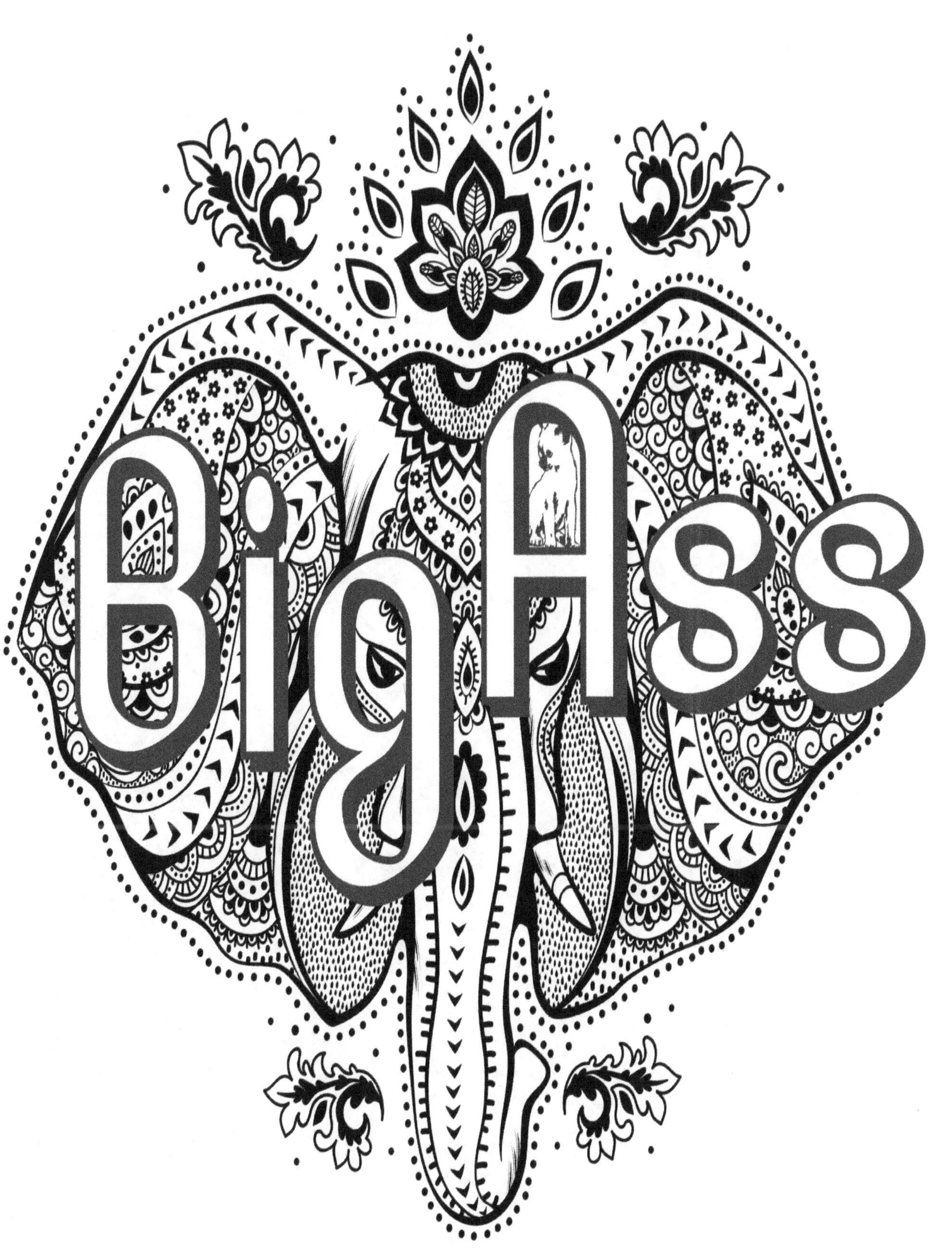
BigAss

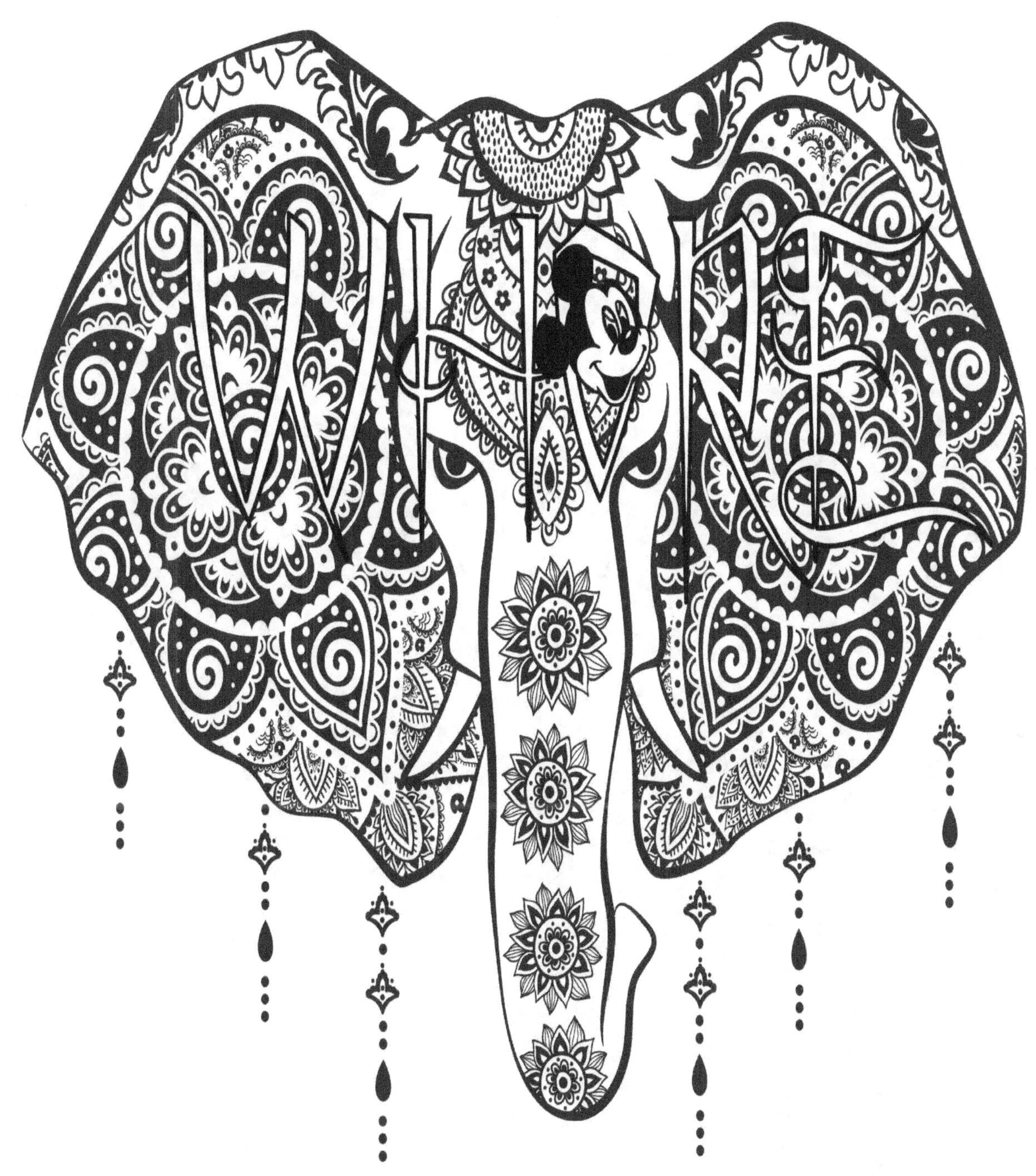

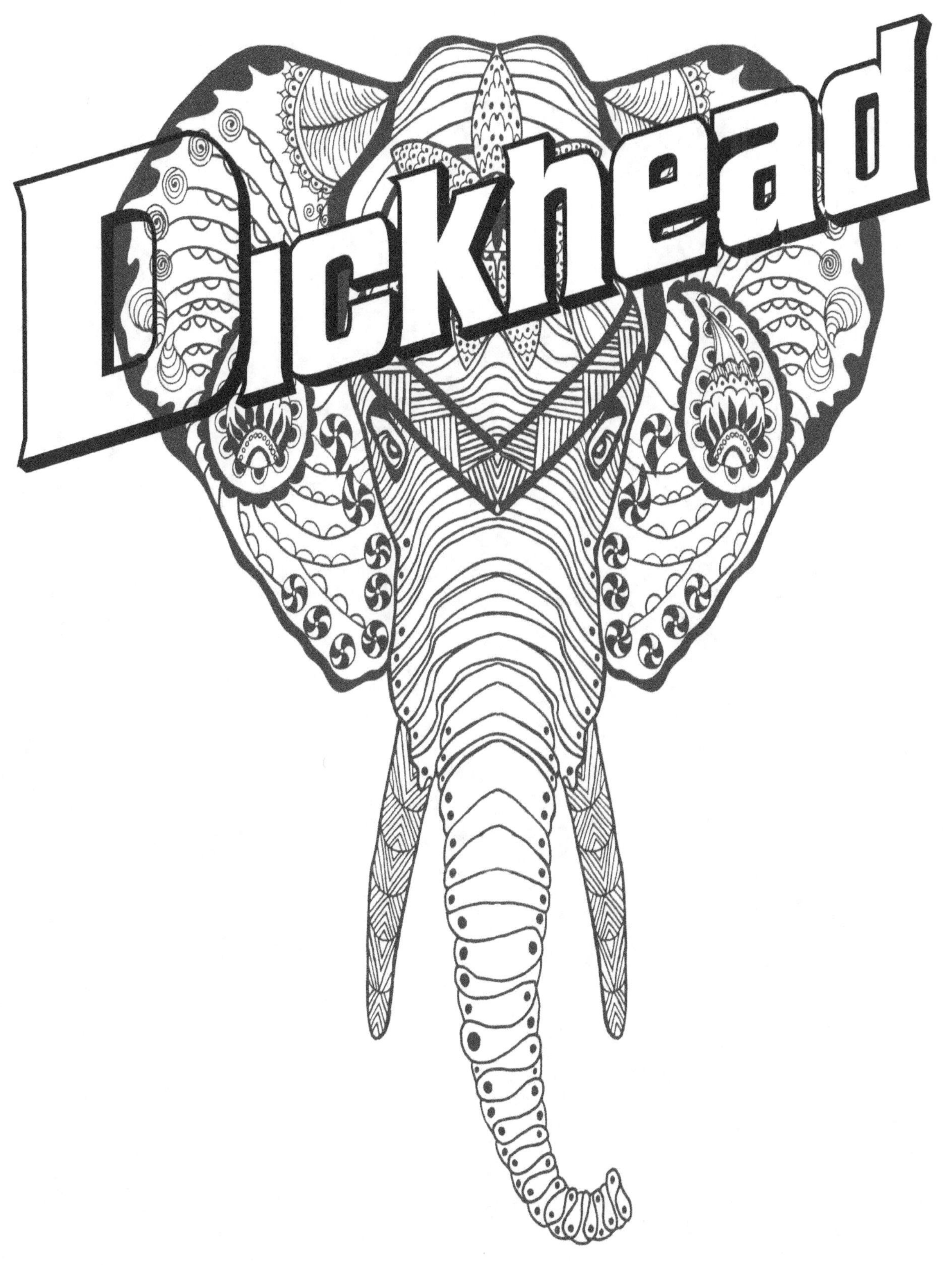

Dickhead

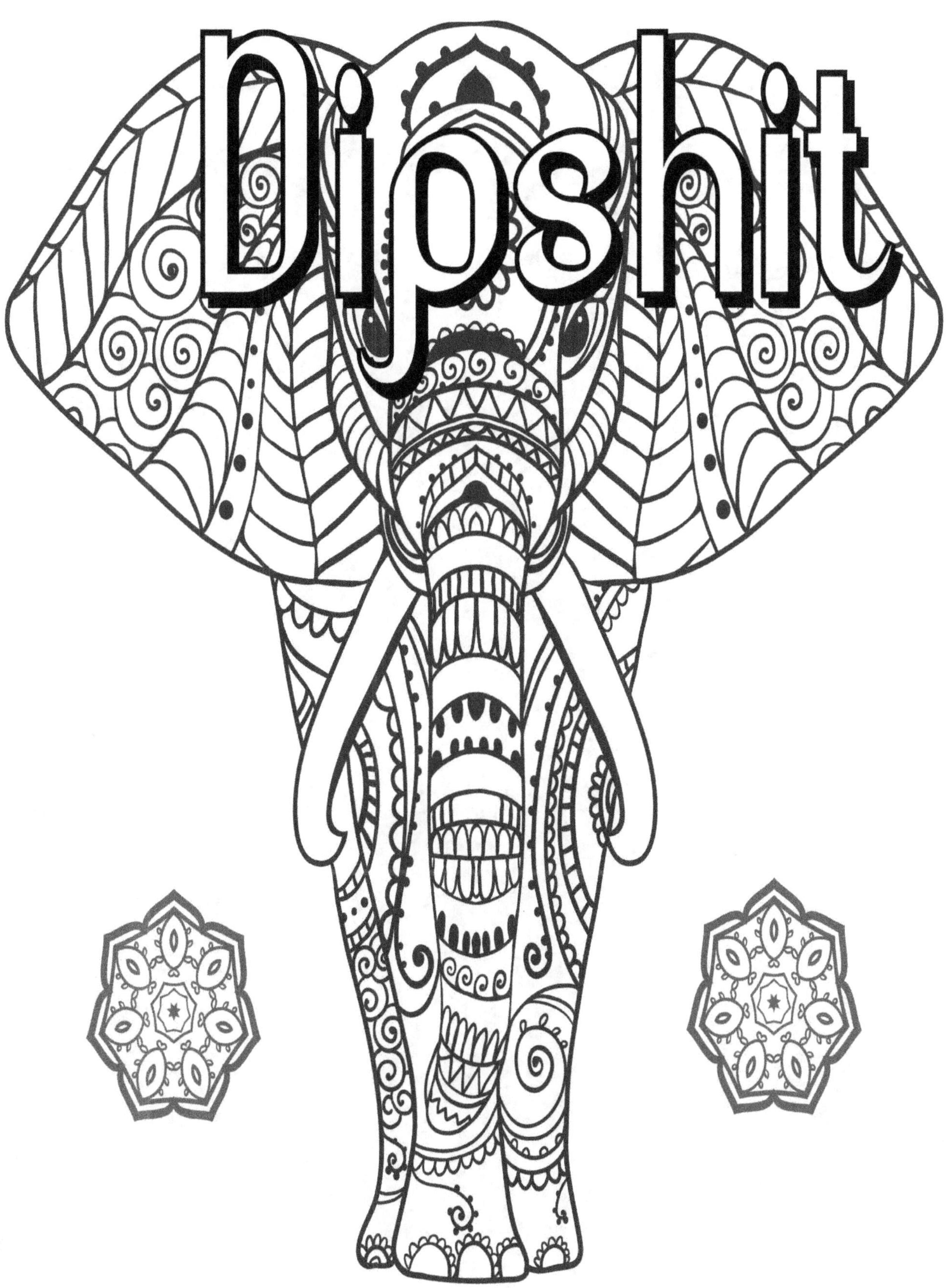

Dipshit

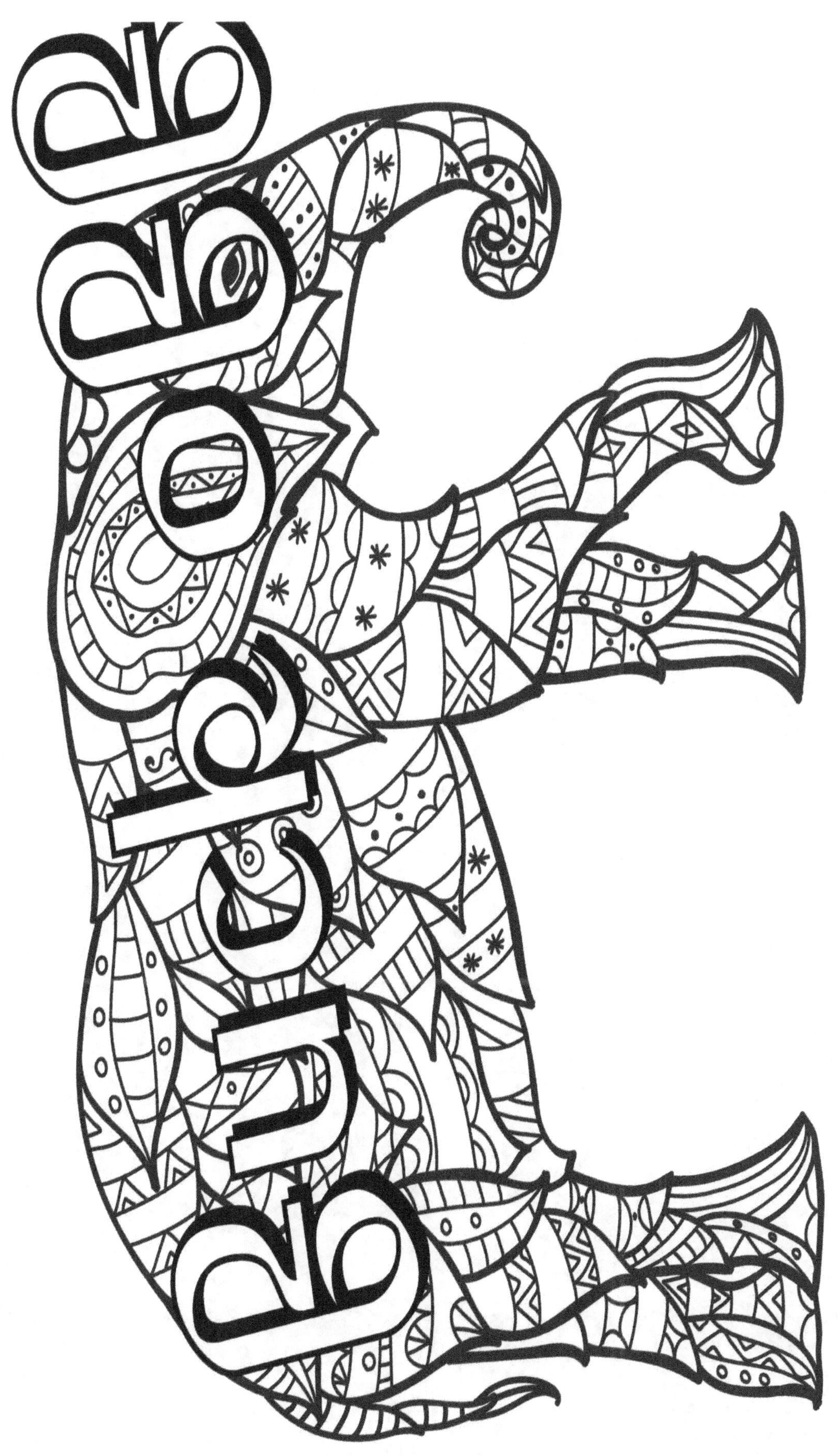